Baby Barnyard

Animals

P9-CKL-023

JAN 2017

Victoria | Vancouver | Calgary

Copyright © 2016 Heritage House Publishing

All rights reserved. No part of this publication may be reproduced, stored in a retrieval system,
or transmitted in any form or by any means—electronic, mechanical, audio recording, or otherwise—
without the written permission of the publisher or a licence from Access Copyright, Toronto, Canada.

Heritage House Publishing Company Ltd.
heritagehouse.ca

CATALOGUING INFORMATION AVAILABLE FROM LIBRARY AND ARCHIVES CANADA

978-1-77203-145-4 (pbk)

Cover design by Jacqui Thomas
Interior book design by Setareh Ashrafologholai
Cover photos by Karnauhov/iStockphoto.com (front) and Anne Conner/iStockphoto.com (back)

Interior photos used by permission of the following, and obtained from **iStockphoto.com**:
DeSid [pig, title page]; man_kukuku [rabbit]; shimmo [donkey]; HABY [swallow];
Paulina Lenting-Smulder [goose]; &#169 William McKelvie [llama]; Craig W. Walsh [Tamworth pig];
Sunitha Pilli [silkworm]; Cindy Singleton [Yorkshire pig]; Jessica & Paul Jones [turkey];
Bernhard Richter [banteng]; AlbyDeTweede [muskox]; Kerstin Waurick [rhea];
Catharina van den Dikkenberg [camel]; Anne Conner [pygmy goat];
and **Shutterstock.com**: Denis Shevyakov [Zebu zow, page 3]; titov dmitriy [duck];
ATGimages [Jacob sheep]; Sue McDonald [Kunekune pig]; Chonlatidphoto [Arabian horse];
Mariusz Szczygiel [cat]; Benedikt Saxier [mule]; Lungkit [chicken]; Vera Zinkova [miniature horse];
Linas T [quail]; Rob kemp [highland cow]; K.A.Willis [emu]; glenda [ankole-watusi]; Goldika [Suffolk sheep];
Steve Meese [shire horse]; Puhach Andrei [border collie]; Jennifer White Maxwell [Guinea fowl];
LeonP [Appaloosa horse]; L F File [fainting goat]; Maria Jeffs [bison]; Perutskyi Petro [honey bee];
Steven Ward [owl]; Polina Truver [yak]; Janice Adlam [angora goat]; Pamela Au [Andalusian horse];
Steven Frame [Nigerian dwarf goat]; Jens Ottoson [water buffalo]; everst [pigeon].

The interior of this book was produced using FSC-certified, acid-free paper,
processed chlorine free and printed with soy-based inks.

We acknowledge the financial support of the Government of Canada through
the Canada Book Fund (CBF) and the Canada Council for the Arts, and the Province of British
Columbia through the British Columbia Arts Council and the Book Publishing Tax Credit.

20 19 18 17 16 1 2 3 4 5

Printed in China

SOME animals live in the wild. Other animals live in our homes as pets. And many animals live on farms or in barnyards. You might know that cows, pigs, sheep, and chickens live on farms. But did you know that these animals come in all sorts of colours, shapes, and sizes? And did you also know that some animals, like mice and owls, usually live in the wild but sometimes make their homes on farms? Dogs and cats are often house pets, but sometimes they have special jobs on farms, like herding sheep or chasing away predators. There are farms all over the world, and some of them might even have animals you have never heard of—like yaks and emus! In this book, you will meet a variety of adorable baby barnyard animals and their parents!

RABBIT

DONKEY

DUCK

JACOB SHEEP

KUNEKUNE PIG

ARABIAN HORSE

CAT

SWALLOW

MULE

GOOSE

LLAMA

CHICKEN

TAMWORTH PIG

MINIATURE HORSE

QUAIL

HIGHLAND COW

EMU

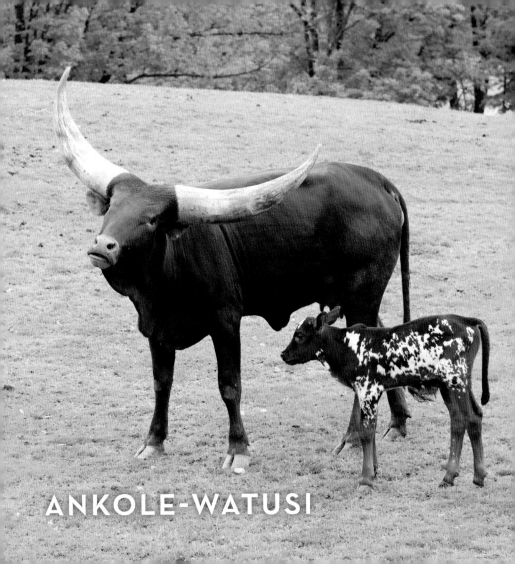

ANKOLE-WATUSI

SUFFOLK SHEEP

SHIRE HORSE

SILKWORM

BORDER COLLIE

GUINEA FOWL

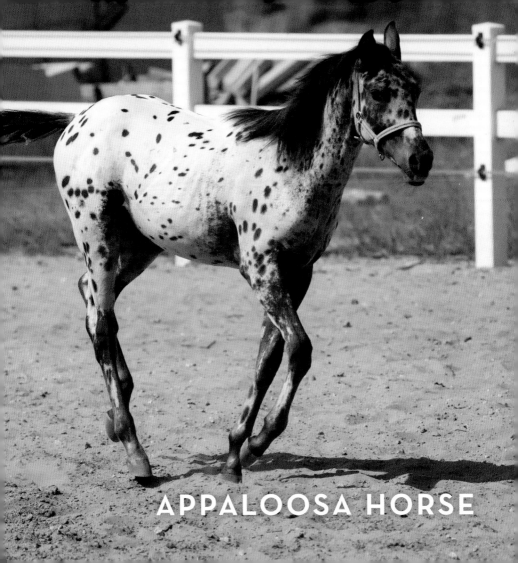

APPALOOSA HORSE

FAINTING GOAT

BISON

HONEY BEE

YAK

ANGORA GOAT

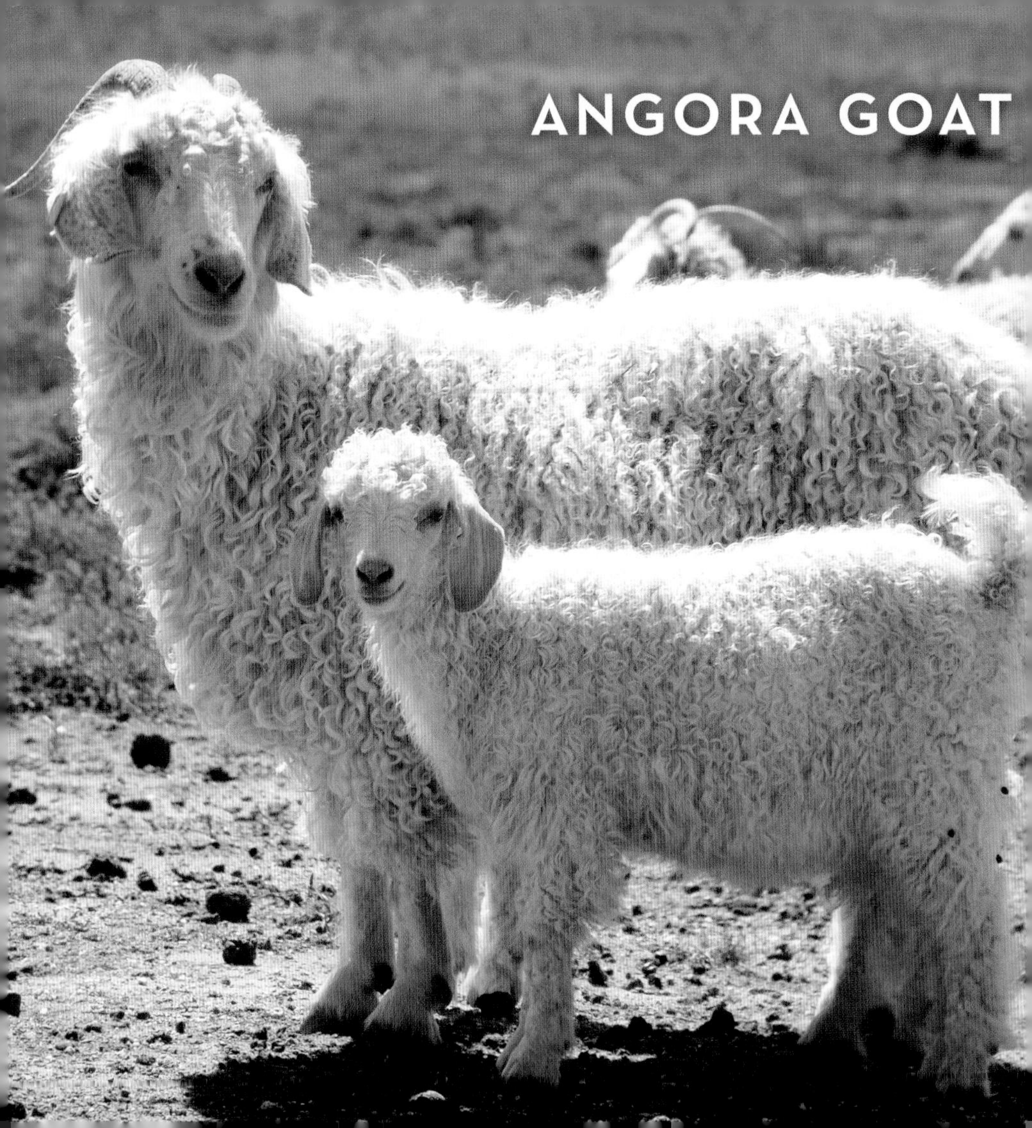

YORKSHIRE PIG

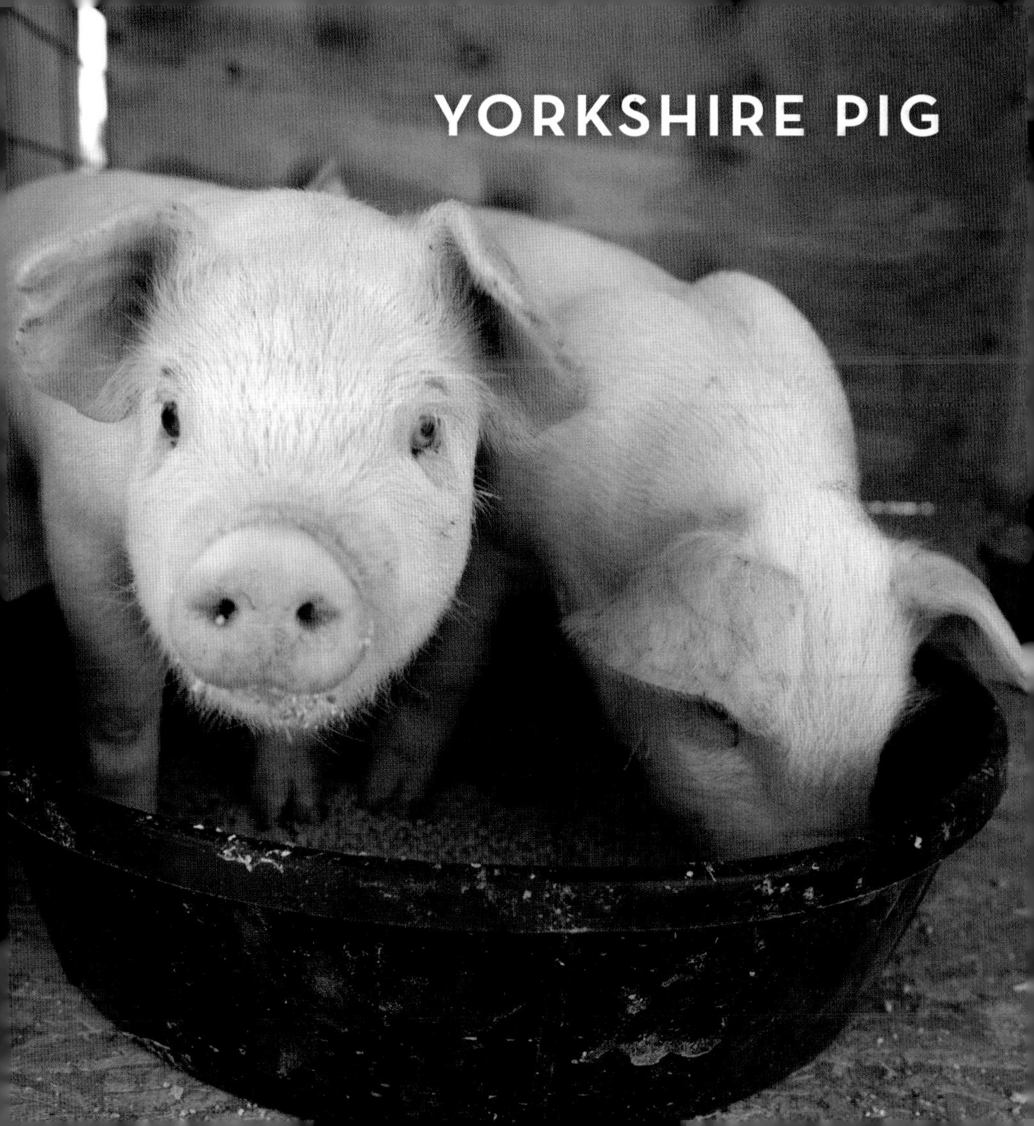

TURKEY

BANTENG

ANDALUSIAN HORSE

MUSKOX

NIGERIAN DWARF GOAT

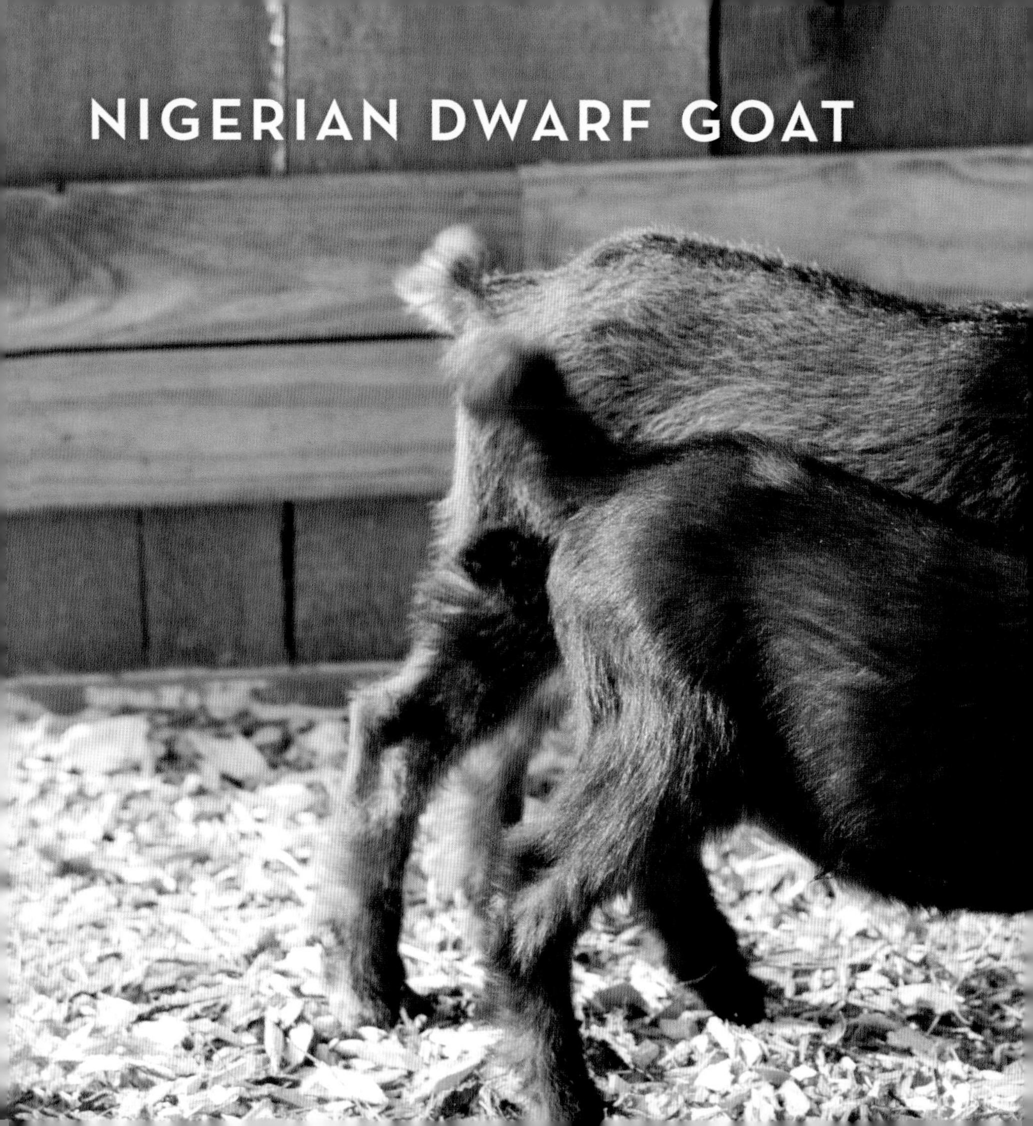

WATER BUFFALO

PIGEON

RHEA

CAMEL

PYGMY GOAT